Ernest Gilliat-Smith

Songs from Prudentius

Ernest Gilliat-Smith

Songs from Prudentius

ISBN/EAN: 9783337006891

Printed in Europe, USA, Canada, Australia, Japan

Cover: Foto ©Thomas Meinert / pixelio.de

More available books at **www.hansebooks.com**

Songs from Prudentius

BY

ERNEST GILLIAT SMITH

JOHN LANE
THE BODLEY HEAD
LONDON AND NEW YORK
1898

CONTENTS

	PAGE
Prologue and Dedication, by the Author	1
Prologue by Prudentius	5
The Cathemerinon.	
A Hymn to Christ	11
At Cock-crowing	19
At Dawn	24
Before Meat	29
After Meat	38
At the Lighting of the Lamps	43
On Going to Rest	50
A Song for those who Fast	56
After Fasting	65
At the Burial of the Dead	69
A Christmas Carol	77
An Epiphany Hymn	83

PROLOGUE AND DEDICATION

Some fifteen hundred years ago,
There dwelt, in sunny Spain, the bard whose praise I hymn;
His name, Prudentius, but of the man, save what he wrote himself

In the brief preface to his work,
Wherein he tells his own life's tale—'Should'st read it friend,—
We naught have cognizance, save this alone, e'en that his voice was sweet.

The musick of it echoes still,
Dim in the mighty vault of Rome's vast sanctuary,
When clerkly voices chant their matin hymn, and sometimes too at night,

And in Toledo's noble shrine—
Where Gothic liturgy, last of its race, still reigns—
When the red sun hath set, and canons sing their old-world evensong.

To make his musick better known,
This is the motive that inspired these halting strains,
Which, model'd in the metres that he used, do show, in
English speech,

The imagery which he conceived,
The thoughts and fantasies, and phantoms that he rais'd,
Anon as he conceived them, and anon embroider'd or curtail'd.

For moods and modes and fancies change,
And sometimes what seem'd sweet two thousand years ago
To-day sounds stern and harsh—grates feeble ears, unused to
minor tones.

But if in aught I've chang'd thy sense,
Or made thee seem to say what thou wouldst not have said,
If thou wert with us now, for this, O glorious bard, I pardon
crave.

II

A debt I owe of gratitude
To one whose patient eyes read and re-read, and read
Again, my manuscript, and what is more, with woman's wit,
advis'd.

To one who taught me first to taste
The silv'ry brightness of thy harp, Prudentius;
To one whom I call wife I dedicate this book of broken rhymes.

III

And, O Prudentius! if still,
Perchance, thou lingerest within the border-land
(And maybe so it is, for in God's sight a thousand years—my God!

A thousand weary, waiting years!—
Hath but the measurement of one short day's brief span),
May the scant off'ring of these harmonies, should Christ accept the gift—

And surely will He condescend,
For though the task of writing them was passing sweet,
Yet doth the smallest gift meet due requitment at His hand, He saith—

Be to thee, for some sort of help,
If not, in very deed, to waft thy spirit on,
Yet leastly, through God's might, for some assuagement in thy waiting time.

But if, perchance, as I would yet
Fain hope, O gentle bard, O valiant Prince, e'en now,
Dost thou regale thy heart in the glad home of God's refulgent Light.

Then whisper, in the Queenly ear,
That Her kind prayers may gain for us—my wife and I,
When the fierce whirling of life's hurricane, at last is hush'd to sleep,

And we have cross'd the mist-clad vale,
(All numb'd with chilling fear) of still Death's frozen shade,
And Time's stern dial hath ceas'd to mark the hours of
winter's blight,

And God's own Spring blooms ev'rywhere,
And Hope's fair fruit is ripe, that we, still hand in hand,
May sun ourselves in thy bright smile and His, our Master's—
Jesus Christ.

SONGS FROM PRUDENTIUS

PROLOGUE

UNLESS memory faileth me,
Since I first saw the light, 'tis seven and fifty years.
For seven and fifty years glad summer's sun hath yearly gladdened me.

And now my course is almost run,
And death, the kinsman of old age, sits close to me.
Throughout all these long years, what have I done worthy of blessedness?

That time of tears and chastisement,
My childhood, I recall once more, and then 'tis youth,
And youth's vain joys, and youth's false follies which rise up before mine eyes.

It shameth me to to think of them—
Those reckless bygone days replete with luxury—
Those days mis-spent which stained mine innocence with strife and wantonness,

Then, to distract my troubled soul,
I set myself to learn the art of government,
And, straightway, emulation strewed my path with thorns and jagged stones.

And then, I knew the sweets of power.
Twice these frail fingers grasped the reins which rule great towns,
Twice I held sovereign sway, and gave men laws, and settled their disputes.

And then, I mounted higher still,
For fortune smiled on me, and I found favour with
My Lord the Emperor, who placed me at his court e'en next himself.

And whilst these things were happening
The white locks of old age stole on me unawares,
And bade me call to mind that I was born when Salias and Philip reigned.

The snow upon my brow doth show
How many winter storms have since swept over me,
How many times since then soft Spring hath passed strewing her rose blossoms.

What profit 's there in earthly things—
Or good or ill—since death must have this earthen vase
And break its feebleness, all which remains of a once noble form?

To me, this may be justly said—
Whosoever thou art, earth's joys are dead to thee,
Those things which thou did'st love are not of God, whose hand shall compass thee.

Then, ere death shall lay hold of thee,
At length, O sinful soul, cast out thy vanity.
Though good deeds thou hast none, yet, with thy tongue, tell of God's clemency.

Let thy days pass in canticles,
And let no night go by which doth not hymn Thy Lord.
Dissipate heresy, sing of His truth, preach Catholic verity.

Fight against all false deities,
And, of her idols purge this mighty town of Rome,
And, for her witnesses, weave thou fair crowns, garlands of hymnody.

And whilst I write or speak these things,
O that these fleshly bonds may break, may be dissolved,
May set my spirit free, that my last sigh may mount in song to Christ !

Songs from Prudentius

SONGS FROM PRUDENTIUS

THE CATHEMERINON:

A HYMN TO CHRIST

I

Hither child, and bring my lyre, and, in faithful strains and true,
I will weave for thee a story, e'en the mighty deeds of Christ.
Him alone my muse shall tell of; Him alone my harp shall hymn.
Christ, Whom David, king and prophet, by God's Spirit all inspir'd,
Joining to his voice the timbrel, and the lute's melodious song,
Sweetest music thus distilling, did foretell in days of yore.
His great deeds I'll lay before thee, tell the legend of His life,
Of its truth the earth bears witness, nor doth earth, what she hath seen
E'en herself, refuse to credit: God Incarnate dwells with men.

II

Of His Father's Heart begotten ere the universe began,
Alpha and Omega call Him: very Fount and Term is He

Of all things which are, and have been, and for evermore
    shall be.
When He spake, they were created; at His word all things
    were made,
Ocean's vastness, earth, and heaven, and the creatures they
    contain,
And the sun, and moon, and planets, floating in the depths of
    space.
He put on man's feeble body, clothed Himself in mortal flesh,
Lest the stock of Adam's children ne'er should see His heavenly
    Face,
Whom a death-charged law had banished to the realms of
    Tartarus.
O that Child-birth truly blessed, when a Virgin Mother, made
Fruitful by God's Holy Spirit, gave Salvation to our race,
When the light of Christ's dear visage for the first time shone
    on man.
Let the firmament of Heaven thunder out its mighty psalm,
And ye sweet-toned Angel-choirs, add to it your antiphon;
Let no creature's tongue keep silence, let all voices jubilate.
For 'tis He of Whom the Sibyl chanted in the days of old;
Whom the prophet's faithful pages to mankind had once
    foretold,
Promised long since, long expected, all Creation hails His
    dawn.

III

See the twelve stone jars at Cana fill'd with rich Falernian;
And the drawers swore 'twas water from the fountain's crystal
    flood,
But the master of the revels praised the raisin's ruby blood.

IV

" I will," He cried, " that thou be cleans'd ; go, show thyself
 unto the priest :
Give the gift which Moses order'd : " and His words were
 ratified ;
As the leper did His bidding, all his flesh grew smooth and
 whole,
And the sadness of his sinning fell from off his stricken soul.

V

Thou, O Christ, dost make sweet ointment with the nectar of
 Thy mouth,
Adding to it grains of healing, which bestoweth Mother
 Earth :
Thus are sightless eyes made seeing, to them thus returns
 God's light.
Thou didst quell the raging tempest whose wild blast lashed
 up the sea :
Fill'd with fear were those frail fishers on the Lake of Galilee :
At Thy word the wind blew softly, and the struggling waves
 lay still.
Lo ! for twelve long years she'd suffered, and on medicine
 spent her all,
Furtively she touched the hemming of Thy sacred outer robe,
And health straightway came back to her, and her cheek grew
 young and fair.

VI

'Twas a widow's only stripling whom the bearers carried out,
And when Jesus saw her anguish, " Youth," He cried, " I say,
 arise."
So in pity gently led him from Death's arms to her embrace.

VII

Lazarus was dead and buried,—four days in the grave had lain,
And the shrine had almost perish'd ere his soul came back again;
Ere the Author of all being ordered him to live once more.

VIII

On the sea, behold Him walking, o'er the billows' foaming crest;
To His steps the swelling waters offer a most solid rest,
Neither do the waves grow weary which His holy Feet have pressed.

IX

Once a man possess'd of devils roamed and raged amid the tombs,
And with fetters oft they bound him, but he always rent his chains,
Till the Lord's Anointed found him, and he fell down at His feet;
Then the unclean throng departed, left the house wherein they dwelt,
Sought another habitation in a herd of grovelling swine,
And they, headlong to the water, perished in the boiling flood.

X

Finish'd were the loaves and fishes, and the guests had gone their way,
" Place," saith He, " in thrice four baskets, all the fragments which now rest."

And five thousand souls had feasted on the bread which Jesus bless'd.
Thou, our Food! our Bread! our Sweetness! Thou, our everlasting Joy!
He who tastes of Thy rich Banquet never hungers, never thirsts,
Doth not sate the wants of nature, cherisheth Eternal Life.

XI

"Ephphetha," He saith, and straightway ears are open'd, tongues are loosed;
Deaf men drink in distant music; dumb men learn at length to speak,
Please themselves with whisper'd converse, and the joys of gentle speech.
See! yon glad youth cloth'd in vigour carrying through the streets his bed;
But just now he lay upon it, pallid, trembling with disease.
It was Jesus Christ Who healed him, at Whose word all sickness flies.
Nay, lest Hell in His salvation never part nor lot should know,
To Hell's very heart He goeth in the bounty of His love;
And Hell's portals bow before Him, and her broken barriers fall,
And that gate, so prompt to ent'rers, stern to them who fain would go,
Swings upon its rusty hinges, and at length gives up its prey;
Night's black threshold now lies open to the footsteps of the dead.
But, whilst God, with golden glory, made Death's cavern bright as day,
Whilst He o'er the startled darkness shed the splendour of His light,

Paled were Æther's stars and mournful, in the lurid atmosphere;
And the sun took flight from Heaven, shrouded deep in fog and mist;
Left his chariot, veiled his brightness, weeping went and hid himself.
Then they say the whole earth shudder'd at the horror of Hell's night.

XII

O my tongue, canst thou keep silence? O my heart, canst thou be still?
Tell the trophy of His Passion, tell the triumph of the Cross!
Sing the glory of the Token signed on ev'ry Christian brow!
Miracle of love stupendous! Wound of new and wond'rous might!
Side by side behold two Fountains, one of Water, one of Blood;
Water for the sinner's cleansing, Blood to buy for him a Crown.
And the Serpent saw the off'ring, saw the Sacred Victim die,
And straightway he lost his power, lost the venom of his bite,
For his head was crush'd for ever, and he hiss'd for very spite.
—Hath it profited thee, Satan, that man's heart thou didst deceive?
That thou whisperedst of the apple in the ear of Mother Eve?
God hath taken human nature, man his loss doth now retrieve.

XIII

Thus it was that Life's great Leader gave Himself awhile to Death.
That dim eyes might grow accustomed, which for long in Hell had groped,

Now that Adam's bonds were broken, to the gladness of God's
  Light.
Then the Patriarchs and Prophets, and a host of holy dead,
Keeping close to their Redeemer as the way to Earth He led,
On the third day found their bodies,—burst all glorious from
  the tomb.
See! rise up from dust and ashes forms of wond'rous loveliness;
Hearts, and bones, and nerves, and sinews, clad in robes of rosy
  flesh,
And the red blood as it courses making their numbed clay to
  glow.
Satan vanquished; Sin forgiven; Man brought back from Hell
  and Night;
To the Throne of His Great Parent, lo! the Conqueror takes
  flight,
And the glory of His Passion maketh Heav'n itself more
  bright.

XIV

Well done! well done! Puissant Monarch! Judge and King
  of Death and Life;
At the Right Hand of Thy Father reign on in Thy power
  and might
Till the Day of Judgment calls Thee sweetly to set all things
  right.
Then let old men's feeble quav'ring mingle with the children's
  choir,
Let the youth and let the virgin join their joyous canticle,
Let young maidens with their mothers raise their simple hearts
  in song,
Let the rushing of the billows as they break against the
  shore,

Let the forests and the meadows and the blossoms of the
 Spring,
And the rain and winds of Autumn, and the heat of Summer's
 glow,
And the cold which bites in Winter, and the hoar frost and
 the snow,
And the day-time, and the night-time, and the sunset and the
 dawn
Make sweet melody together—laud Thy Name for evermore!

AT COCK CROWING

I

THE herald bird which haileth day
Hath sounded his shrill clarion,
'Tis Christ, the soul's awakener,
Recalling man once more to life.

Away, He cries, with sickly sleep,—
Soft, slothful, deathlike, desident,
Be pure and sober and upright,
And watch, for I am near at hand.

'Twill be too late to leave thy bed
When the bright Sun speeds on his way,
Unless kind Night hath given thee
Some time to labour and to pray.

The birds which nest beneath the eaves
Flutter their wings at dawn and sing;
Then let their voices be for thee
The trumpet of thy Lord and King,

Which bids thee, wreathed and lulled by dreams,
Put off thy slumber and thy sleep,
Spring from thy couch, and vigil keep,
Now that the Daylight draweth nigh.

So shall Aurora, when with tears
All glistening, she dews the sky,
Confirm thee with the hope of day,
Who toiledst ere she showed her face.

This Sleep, which God bestows in time,
Is but the type of timeless Death,
And Sin's dark canopy, like Night,
Shuts out the beauty of His Light.

So Christ's clear Voice rings out on high,
Forewarning men His Day is near,
Imploring them, in accents sweet,
To quit the servitude of Sleep,

Lest she until the very end,
Of lives misspent in idleness,
Should steep and bury them in sin,
All heedless of the coming Light.

II

At Night foul fiends and phantoms prowl,
Rejoicing in the darkling mist,
But when the cock crows, so men say,
Trembling, they flee in wild dismay,

For, then, they know that Day is near,
That soon above their heads shall shine
The glory of the Light Divine
Which scattereth Hell's dark satellites.

They know too, 'tis the sign of Hope—
The symbol of Man's one great Hope—
The Hope, by which he, roused from sleep,
Beholds the Coming of his King.

III

How puissant this winged creature's might
The Christ in Peter's fall doth show.
"Me thrice," He saith, "shalt thou deny
Or 'ere the cock at dawn shall crow.

And Peter stained his soul with fear
Before the messenger of day,
Whose clarion driveth night away,
Had ushered in the rosy dawn.

But when those shrill notes thrilled his ears,
Forthwith he mourned with bitter tears
The dread which made pale lips belie
That faith his soul so staunchly held.

But never more, with slippery tongue,
Such words of weakness did he say,
Nor sinned again, when he had heard
The crowing of God's herald bird.

IV

So too, as old world legend tells,
'Twas at that quiet hour of night
At which the cock exultant crows,
That Christ came back from Tartarus.

Then was death's tyranny o'erthrown,
Then was Hell's power broken quite,
Then Day, rejoicing in his might,
Scattered for aye the clouds of night.

Now let all evil things lie still,
And struggling wickedness have rest,
And lethal punishment o'erwhelmed
Be lulled to sleep on night's own breast.

But he who looks for Christ's approach
Springs from his couch at dawn of day,
Before the night has reached her goal,
And watches till his Lord shall come.

O Jesu, Lord, we cry to Thee,
Mourning we lift our hands to Thee,
For earnest prayer and vigilant
Forbiddeth the pure heart to sleep.

Too long hath deep Oblivion,
Encompassing this fragile frame,
Opprest and weighed down and o'erwhelmed
The wand'ring mind with empty dreams.

For all that's done for earthly gain
Is false and frivolous and vain,
Like actions dreamed about in sleep.
Awake! awake! for Truth is here.

Gold, luxury, and sinful mirth,
Wealth, honours, and prosperity,
Before His Light shall melt away,
Like night-clouds at the break of Day.

Lord Jesu! rouse our souls from Sleep,
And break the bonds of Mist and Night,
And loose the fetters forged by Sin,
And fill us with Thy new-born Light.

AT DAWN

I

BEGONE, O clouds and mist and gloom,
Confused and troubled things of earth,
Light is at hand, the heaven grows white,
Christ draweth nigh, give place O night.

Earth's sable robe is reft in twain,
Pierced by the sun god's golden spear,
And when the day star kissed the plain,
Her pallid cheek grew red again.

Anon the mist which blinds these eyes
Shall melt before God's rosy dawn,
Then shall the clouds of darkness break,
And all things own His sovereignty.

Then every secret shall be solved,
And every hidden thing laid bare,
Then shall the beauty of His light
Enlighten every mystery.

II

Concealed beneath night's azure veil
The lurking robber sins at ease,
But, when he sees the light of day,
With trembling steps he slinks away.

So crafty error, shrewd and sly,
Rejoiceth in obscurity,
So impure spirits find their rest,
Lapped in the shame of night's pale breast.

Behold the blazing sun arise!
It irks, it shames, it sorrows them,
For no man can remain in sin
On whom have shone His beaming eyes.

For passion's fever then dies down,
Then the stained robe grows fair and white.
Who in the morning will not weep
For what he did mid sin's dark night?

III

This hour is welcome unto all,
For each one now may ply his trade,—
The soldier and the toga'd judge
The sailor and the husbandman,

The merchant and the man of toil.
Forensic glory, fame in war,
Or thirst for gain, or very need,
These are the spurs which drive them on.

But we, of speech, and place, and wealth,
And warlike arts, are ignorant.
E'en Thee, O Christ, alone we know,
And the sweet folly of Thy cross.

Thee, with pure souls and simple hearts,
With prayer and holy canticle,
On bended knees we learn to seek,
Mingling our tears with hymnody.

This is our profit, this our gain,
By this chaste art alone we live,
This is the service which we pay
With the first gleam of dawning day.

O God examine well my heart,
And search out all mine intellect.
How many are the stains and blots
Which thy clear light shall purify!

O may I shine as then I shone,
When, at the bidding of Thy word,
I washed away sin's leprosy
In Holy Jordan's healing stream.

And whatsoe'er since that glad day
Earth's night hath plunged in darkling mist
Do Thou, O bright and Morning Star,
With thy sweet smile illuminate.

O Thou, Who makest crimson white,
And ebony of crystal hue,
And pitch black stains as fair as milk
Most Holy One, e'en cleanse me too.

IV

'Twas neath the purple haze of night
That Jacob with an angel strove,
Nor did the ill-matched combat cease
Until the sun began to shine.

Then, when his splendour filled the sky,
The Patriarch went halt and lame,
For Heavenly might had touched his thigh,
And put his vaunted strength to shame.

He lost the will and power to sin
With the first ray of dawning light.
Behold a parable herein,
A parable of wrong and right.

These figures teach the heart, that man,
Sown in the darkness of sin's shade,
Unless he freely yield to God,
Shall one day lose his rebel strength.

More blessed he whom Dawn shall find
For Christ's sake, maimed and mortified—
With eye plucked out, or hand, or foot,
Aye cut off quick, and cast aside.

V

Let darkness now, at length, depart,
That gruesome and perfidious gloom
Which long hath veiled these blinded eyes,
And led these erring steps astray.

May this, Christ's Light, His peace bestow,
And render us for Him most pure,
And may our lips speak nothing false,
And may our hearts conceive no guile.

So may we pass the whole day through,
That neither tongue, nor hand, nor eye,
Nor luxury, nor love of self,
Shall separate our souls from God.

He is the Searcher of all hearts,
He spieth out each hidden thing,—
All that we think, or do, or say,
From sunrise until evensong.

He is the Witness, He the Judge,
He seeth whatsoever is.—
Whate'er the human heart conceives,
And none can brave His scrutiny.

BEFORE MEAT

I

FOUNDER of all things, Thou Incarnate Word,
Born in late time of a Virgin most pure,
Yet still with Jehovah or ever were laid
Earth's vast foundations or Ocean's deep bed,
O gentle Crucifer, Sower of Light.

Hither, come hither, with health-giving rays,
Bend down the beauty of Thy beaming smile,
That of the gifts which God's kind care hath given,
We may partake to the glory of Heaven,
Sealed with the signet of Thy Holy Name.

Without Thy favour all sweetness is gall,
E'en honey and nectar but roughen the mouth,
But when Thou hast looked on them, harsh things grow mild,
The bread of affliction is bitter to eat,
But when Thou hast blest it, the bitter grows sweet.

O may my bread savour and taste of God's Love,
May Christ in His kindliness imbue my cup,
And may the gentle Dove brood o'er my board,
E'en so, shall Charity,—Threefold—Divine,
Purify,—sanctify, feasters and feast.

II

I'll not spoil the rose bush to garnish my hall,
Nor burn precious spices to laden the air,
Ambrosial odours and nectar most rare,
Rained straight down from heaven like manna of old,
Shall perfume my table and nourish my guests.

Look down, O my muse, on the ivy's light spray,
And rob not Silenus to crown thy chaste brow,
But weave of fair dactyls, as well thou know'st how,
To the glory of Him from Whom all blessings flow,
Garlands of hymnody—strophes of praise.

No labour more noble can nourish thine art,
Sweet sister of musick, whose generous soul
Was born of pure Æther and God's golden Light,
Than to hymn the grand Giver of every good gift—
To praise the great Lord and Creator of all—

God who hath fashioned all creatures for man,
Which earth, sky or water doth bring forth and rear.
The beasts of the field, and the fowls of the air,
And the myriad-fold life which vast ocean doth breed,
All these hath he set neath the stern heel of man,

Whose cunning outsoareth the eagle's swift flight,
And pierceth the depths of Leviathan's home.
See crafty snares compass the forest and hill,
Lay wait in the woodland, and lurk side the rill
Take tribute and tithing of God's feathered flock.

Lo, nets draw their toils through the heart of the sea,
And subtle hooks tender the temptingest baits
In streamlet, and river, and mill pond, and brook,
Entangle a host of God's wave wandering folk,
Befool the frail stomachs of truculent fish.

And Earth, too, doth bring forth her riches innate,
Tokens of favour and blessing divine,
The fruit of her vineyards, and golden-eared wheat,
And unction of olives with healing replete,
The wealth of her corn, and her oil, and her wine.

O wealth which outshineth the gleaming of gold !
O wealth which bestoweth on man angel's food,
And chalice containing Salvation's own price,
And ointment for pardon, and blessing, and strength,
Christ's Holy Mysteries need nothing more.

Far be it from me, then, to lust after blood—
Sure seed of envy and hatred and strife,
To feed carnal fire by feasting on flesh,
To make myself bestial by slaughtering beasts.
These things befit not the servants of Christ.

A pottage of lentils, a crust of wheat bread,
A handful of herbs which my garden bestows,
Ripe fruit which drops down like rain from the tree—
Lies prone on the grass plot all purple and gold
Or milk-white and crimson, as rubies and pearls.

Nectar-like honey which droppeth as dew
From Amber-hued cells of virginal comb,
Savours of heather, and hare-bells, and thyme,
Work of that restless purveyor the bee,
Who knows not of wedlock the pangs nor the sweets.

Goblets all foaming with milk, white as snow,
Gift of my ewe lambs, and gentle she goats,
You may churn it to butter, or curd it to cheese,
Lo these things afford me an innocent feast—
Chaste viands for Christians, a banquet for men.

Minstrels of old could not praise thee enough,
The wealth of their psalteries and trumpets and shawms,
E'en added the sweetness of David's own harp,
Welded together in one mighty psalm,
Would ne'er, were the harmony never so rich,
Balance the riches God raineth on man.

Thee, then, O Father, when day is new born,
And when the sun hath run one half his course,
And when his waning torch shedding soft light
Calleth the weary to meat and to rest,
Shall the frail tones of my harmonies hymn.

And that Thou hast given us breath to proclaim,
A heart which exultant can tremble and throb,
A throat, and a palate, a voice, and a tongue,
To fashion fair language, and coin gentle song,
For this do we render thanksgiving and praise.

III

Us, then, O Holy One, bearing in mind
The mantle of purple Thou one day wouldst wear,
Thy right hand didst build up and fashion of clay,—
Image and pattern of Thy sacred form,
Perfect with spirit which came forth from God.

Then, in a garden of holy delights,
Where timber primeval shed peace and sweet shade,
Where water all crystal in four living streams,
Made glad gentle pastures, bespangled with flowers,
And spring ever breathed out the scent of her grace,

With joy and rejoicing Thou badest us dwell.
" All these," said Jehovah, I give for thy use,
And ev'ry creature shall serve thy delight,
But see that thou pluck not, the fruit of the tree,
Whose grand limbs rise threatening mid Eden's fair bowers."

"It's apples are Hell-charged, and bitter as death."
And when Satan heard Him, he coiled all his craft
Around the fell beauty of that fatal tree,
With look, and with gesture, and subtly-laid speech,
Befooled the proud frailty of Eve's froward heart.

She stretched out her right hand, she plucked and did eat,
She gave to her husband, and he too did eat.
Such was the sowing of sorrow, and sin.
Stript of the mantle of God's Holy Grace,
Of nakedness swift have they knowledge and fear,

Fashion of fig leaves a shield for their shame,
Flee 'fore the voice of God, exiled from home,
Whilst Eve, who before was unshackled and free,
Must needs bend her neck 'neath the yoke of man's love,
Experience of wedlock, the thorns and the stings.

And Satan, the founder and father of guile,
Foul serpent who breathed out the poison of sin,
Is crippled for ever, abashed and bound down—
" The Woman subservient to Man all Divine,
Shall crush 'neath her heel e'en thy triple-tongued head."

From such sorry sowing there sprang up a crop
Blasted and blighted in blossom and bud,
Rash as their mother—weak-kneed as their chief,
Heaping on infamy sin after sin,—
Earning the wages of wickedness—Death.

But see now, there bursts forth, at length, a new stock,
A new Adam sent down from God's golden Light,
Not as the old Adam, earthy, of earth,
Yet made in every way like unto him,
Save without bodily weakness and sin.

Conceived not of man's will, nor love's squalid rite,
Nor through the bondage of wedlock's dire chains,
Word of Jehovah incarnate is He,
E'en through the glistering might of God's grace,
Born of a Virgin, immaculate, free,
True God of True God for man's sake made man.

And that the serpent all prone on God's earth
Lay now crushed and bleeding 'neath Eva's fair foot,
This was the cause of the time-honoured hate,
Of the feud, fierce and bloody, more cruel than death,
Of the war ever waging 'twixt her seed and his.

For she who was worthy to bring forth her God,
Doth tame ev'ry evil and vanquish all vice,
And he, green with envy, in impotence writhes,
Breathes threatening vainly, deprived of his sting,
Vomits out venom as harmless as milk.

What savage demon doth not tremble now,
Scared at the whiteness of Christ's ransom'd flock?
What rabid weir wolf forgetful of blood,
But wanders not mournful amid dauntless sheep,
Fearing to open his pitiless fangs.

O grand alteration, O marvellous change,
Proud lions now cringe 'fore the Lamb which was slain,
The Dove that descended from God's glowing light,
Doth scatter the eagles, and put them to flight,
Doth drive them through storm-cloud and whirlwind to Hell.

O Christ, Thou for me art that most Mighty Dove,
'Fore whom flee those fierce fowl, made drunk with man's blood,
Thou for me, O my Jesu, art that snow-white Lamb
Who bendeth the tiger's proud neck 'neath Thy yoke,
And who from the sheepfold doth ward off the wolf.

O God, rich in bounty, grant this to Thy flock,
Invoking Thy Holy Name duly in prayer—
To brace with frugality, chasten, refresh,
Digestion made easy, with light meat and drink,
Lest sickness and gluttony strangle the soul.

Forbidden fruit breedeth the sure seeds of fire,
Appetite sated inflameth desire,
Bitter the taste of the revel at dawn.
Far be it from me, then, with wine-cup and feast,
To waken the slumbering embers of sin.

Enough for the serpent—alack and a-day—
That apples unholy should once have bred vice.
Enough that God's handiwork, made like to him,
Should once bend the neck beneath gluttony's yoke,
Once drink the poison which bringeth forth Death.

Yet, work of thy breathing, Lord, man's vital spark
Shall ne'er see corruption and never know Death,
Word-like from God's gracious lips coming forth,
Swift from the glowing of His fiery throne,
The light of pure reason sustaineth her life.

Nay, bodies too, reparation shall find,
E'en though Time's fingers should fret them to dust,
Arrayed in new beauty the old forms shall rise,
Brought back from Death's ashes, and Winter's dead sleep—
Fair flow'rets, bursting to life with God's Spring.

For surely I know—and no vain hope is this—
Life's husk shall anon share its lost comrade's lot,
Bethink thee how easily Jesu came back
From the dread surging of Phlegethon's gloom,
Glad with a host of revivified dead.

And this hope remaineth alike to my bones,
Destined to slumber awhile in the grave,
To rest for a season in Earth's soft embrace ;
For Jesus our leader, who trod the same path,
Will call me anon to His home 'mid the stars.

AFTER MEAT

I

FRAGILE Nature cried out, faint for refreshment,
And of God's gracious gifts have we partaken
O my tongue pay thy debt—Hymn God who fed thee.

'Fore whom glad cherubim cry out in rapture,
And white-robed Seraphim fall down and worship,—
Chant their Trishagion, for aye and ever.

Creator of all things, and Earth's great Founder,
No beginning hath He, nor hath He ending,
Lord God of Sabaoth, this is His title.

Limpid Fountain of Life, from God's heart flowing,
One Infuser of Faith, His pureness sowing,
Mighty Binder of Death, all health bestowing,

We in Christ live and move and have our being.
Wondrous token of love, their Hearts uniting,
With these twain reigns the Dove, from both proceeding,

Whose clear whiteness descends to earthen vessels,
Comes to man's rugged soul, when man will have Him—
If his dour heart but give a smile of welcome.

But should aught of deceit or squalour enter
There where once the fair Dove found grateful refuge,
As from shrine desecrate, forth swift He flieth.

For where guilt seething lies within the bosom,
Swart with foul vapour burns Fear's sick flame quiv'ring,
And black Panic repels the Dove's soft brooding.

Would'st thou in thy poor heart build up a temple,
In which Christ's love could rest in peace for ever?
Keep thy conscience then clean from sin's pollution,

And court white Innocence with fond desire,
And in thy meat and drink be ever frugal.
So shalt thou guard thyself from gloom and sickness;

So shalt thou fit thy heart to welcome Jesus,
God's own heaven-born Bread rained down to feed thee,
More melting to the mouth than Israel's manna,

And sweeter to the tongue than virgin-honey.
O God, all praise be Thine, nutrition twofold
Doth thus through love refresh both soul and body.

II

So, too, in days of yore, Thy might precluent
Mid the hoarse lion's roar, a man did cherish
With twofold feast sent down in tender pity.

Him (Bel's cast brazen mien and might contemning,
To bow 'fore his great shrine and offer blessing,
So own his right divine, all stark refusing),

Proud Babylon's fierce king, with anger raging,
E'en to Death's jaws decreed, and lions rending,
An hunger'd for his flesh—for heart's blood thirsting.

O Faith, O Piety! Christ guards ye ever!
The savage lions cringe and fawn upon him,
And lick his hands and face with tongues unbloody,

And of fierce hunger's lust and pangs forgetful,
They down beside him lie, all tamed and gentle,
And bend their shaggy crests for his caresses.

And when he, shut up there, with famish'd comrades
For six long weary days, himself grew hungry,
And raised weak hands to God, whose love had saved him,

God sent a messenger to earth from Heaven,
To cheer His sore-tried friend with food and comfort.
Who swiftly to Judea, like lightning, flying,

There 'spied old Habacuc the prophet, bearing
To his good reaping folk a homely dinner,
Which he himself had boiled with bread and lentils.

And, stretching out his deft right hand, the Angel seized him,
Bore him o'er hill and dale, o'er stream and woodland,
Across the mighty plain, to Bab'lon's city.

Gently there set him down o'er 'gainst the lions,
And then old Habacuc, all breathless, trembling,
In broken quav'ring speech cried out to Daniel,

Whose eager hands received the reapers' dinner.
" O thou servant of God," thus spake the prophet,
" Take this, that God hath sent thee through his Angel,

And for His timely aid give thanks to Heaven.
Then Daniel, when his heart with meat was gladdened,
Fill'd with new life and hope, raised up his eyelids.

" Amen," said he, " Amen and Alleluia."
So too we, gracious Lord, who givest all things—
Whose tend'rest love and kindly Hand hath fed us,

Would make our act of praise,—our *Deo gratias*.
For harassed sore were we, befoul'd and slander'd,
Turned on the cruel spit of Satan's malice.—

God's Faith is e'er the butt of spite and envy—
Deep in World's dungeon bound, weighed down by matter
We too lay fainting, parch'd—no food, no water,

And seven huge beasts of prey, with ceaseless raging,
Prowl'd o'er our prison-house, alert for booty,
And Thou, our only hope, when we invoked Thee,

Closed the fierce lions' jaws, and hushed their fury,
And, with Thine own fair flesh, didst cheer and feed us.
Naught shalt those find more mild, naught more refreshing,

Naught, to thine ears, all numb'd with Satan's roaring,
More comely, cheering, kind, replete with healing,
Than the prophetic voice of God's Priest, massing.

O feast surpassing sweet, O daintiest banquet!
O Bread from Heaven sent! O Cup of Blessing!
Drink deep poor thirsty soul, and sate thine hunger.

And when thou'st had thy fill, all calm and tranquil,
Let tyrants raging howl, and judge thee wrongly,
Let lions, if they will, aye tear and rend thee.

Naught shall make thee deny thy Lord and Master—
That He is throned on High with God His Father;
For with a gladsome heart His Cross thou'lt carry.

AT THE LIGHTING OF THE LAMPS

I

FOUNDER and Leader and Lord of the Golden Light,
Who time from time dost part by seasons sure and fix'd,
The sun hath sunk to rest, and night draws on apace,
Shed thy bright beams abroad o'er all Thy faithful race.
Although with countless stars Thou paintest all the sky,
And in Thy royal Hall dost hang a lunar lamp,
Yet dost Thou bid us seek our light from steel and flint,
And cherish seeds of flame, bred of the stricken rock.
For, thus, shall all men know their hope of life lies hid
In Christ's own sacred Form, His Body and His Blood;
He is the solid Rock whence cometh man's sole Light.
The new-born flame we nurse in little earthen lamps
Fill'd with the luscious juice which olive fruit distils,
Unless a pine torch tends its puny flick'ring life,
Or some tall, straight bull-rush cut from the river bank
And steeped in flower-born wax where honey once lay hid.
It lives, the quiv'ring flame—or lamp, or res'nous torch,
Or rounded comb-clad rush the vital heat bestow—
And grows and waxeth strong, a brilliant, shim'ring light.
See, from the glowing top sweet nectar trickles down,
Like gently falling tears, for fiery might doth make
A molten stream to well around the dripping wick.

G—2

Thus all Thy courts, O God, through Thy Paternal grace,
Glister with gladsome Light which emulates glad Day,
And, as before his rays, black Night, with robe all rent,
Shrouds her pale conquer'd head, and cringing slinks away.

II

Who doth not know the swift Light's lofty origin,—
That the pure source from whence it flows is God alone.
When Moses saw His Glory, in the days of old,
It beamed from forth a bush, all clad in flames of gold.
Thrice happy he, to whom Jehovah thus made known
His heaven-born healing Light, around that sacred thorn,—
He, whom God bade to let his feet, all shoeless, rest,
Lest they should soil the ground which that pure Light had blest.

III

A race of noble blood, strong in their sire's might,
But 'neath a tyrant's heel long held in slavery,
That same fair Heaven-born Light doth shelter and make free,
Doth pilot, and doth guide through wilderness and sea.
With scintillating beams, brighter than noon-day sun,
Before their watchful eyes its splendour ever shines.
Through all that desert land it gilds their weary way,
And makes the azure night, for them, as clear as day.

IV

There is a far-off land, whose fields and fertile plains
Are watered by a river which men call the Nile,

'Twas there the race of whom I sing were held as slaves,
And, when at length they fled, the king who ruled that land—
Beneath whose cruel lash their backs had oft-times bled,
Was cut with bitter grief, aye to the very quick,
And, filled with rage, he summoned all his soldiery,
And ordered them to join with him in swift pursuit.
The braying trumpet sounds the mournful note of war,
Men fly to arms and gird themselves with threatening knives,
And women weep, all trembling for their loved ones' lives,
And banners flaunt, and horses prance, and chariots roar.

v

And now, the people, who had toiled 'neath Egypt's sun,
Had clean forgot the hardships of their servitude,
For lo, they see the purple of the distant waves,
And soon upon the ruddy shore sit down to rest.
Anon the cry goes up that Pharaoh's host is near,
And, with its mighty chief, is threatening war and death.
But Moses was unmoved, "Fear not, go forth," said he,
"Your path before you lies, straight through the stormy sea."
Forthwith the waters part—roll up on either side
Huge banks of swelling waves, like walls of malachite;
Between them, smooth and firm, a road of golden sand,
And thither Israel wends his way, 'twixt sea and sea.
And Egypt's swarthy crew and Egypt's impious king,
Burning with bitter hate,—greedy for Hebrew blood,
E'en dare to follow him beneath the beetling flood,
To tread the fatal path which Jacob's feet had trod.
The royal squadrons, egged on by the noise and whirl,
Rush headlong through the waves, and then, the waters fall,—
Fall down on them with all their mingled mightiness,
And rend, and throttle them, like savage beasts of prey.

Behold them vainly struggling with their wat'ry foe,
Behold the wreckage of that valiant fighting host,
The flower of Egypt's manhood strewn on Egypt's coast,
And all the lordly land of Pharaoh plunged in woe.

VI

What tongue duly can sing Thy glory and Thy praise,
O Christ, Thou Lord and Chief, Who with a mighty hand
And stretched-out arm didst free thy servant Israel
From cruel servitude—from Pharao's tyranny?
O Thou, Who didst hold in vast ocean's struggling waves,
That 'mid two walls of sea, with Thee to pilot him,
Jacob might safely pass through their mysterious home,
And that their fury then should fall on Egypt's host!
O Thou, for Whom the dry rocks gush out gurgling streams,—
For Whom the cleft crag pours clear water fresh and cool,
Which, prattling like some silv'ry brook 'mid shady banks
And flower-strewn plains, doth quench thy way-worn children's thirst!
O Thou for Whom the gall like drink of Mara's pool,
Healed by a tree laid low grows sweet as honeycomb!—
O mighty tree—which makes all bitter things taste sweet!
O glorious blood-stained tree, whence all our hope doth flow!—
O Thou for Whom the camp is filled with snow-white food
Which glides down swiftly, like hoar frost in winter time,
Straight from the star-lit sky! 'Twas thus with angels' bread,
O Christ, Thou comfortedst Thy people's famished hearts.
For Thee the south wind blows—the wind which bringeth rain,
And driveth up from 'yond the sea huge flocks of quails,

Which, cast down to the earth, cannot take flight again.
Thus in due season didst Thou give Thy children meat.

VII

And all these glorious gifts, once to our forefathers,
His wondrous love bestowed, Who liveth God alone,
By whose kind succour we, too, taste the heav'nly feast,
And thus with mystic bread nourish our famish'd souls.
He for us stills the storm,—man's gracious Arbiter,
Who from earth's dread quicksands, beckoning weary souls—
Toil-toss'd and footsore, worn out with life's travailing,
Bids them go up to the Home of the Righteous,
Where, veiled with purple roses, all the land is fragrant,
Where living fountains well and flow in crystal streams,
Wat'ring with limpid spray amber-hued marigolds,
And golden crocus flow'rs, and tender violets.
Where sweet balsam, distill'd from many a tiny branch,
Runs down the mighty trunks of all the forest trees,
Where spices, rare and choice, laden the scented air,
Where floats the spikenard leaf which from its hidden source
The gliding river bears to ocean's boundless waves.
O too happy they, who through meadows green and fair,
O'er snow-white lilies, lead their steps in innocence,—
Who all with one accord, raising their clear voices,
Make Heaven re-echo, fill'd with sweet harmony.

VIII

And e'en to the lost souls our God shows His pity.
Days free from suffering oftentimes gladden them.

Thus on the Night when from Acheron's sad waters
To breathe earth's living air, Life's Lord comes back again—
Not like to Lucifer rising from Ocean,
Who with a kindling torch bids night and mist give place,
But o'er this land of tears, than the sun's might greater,
From the Cross on which He died new daylight shedding—
With gentle punishment Tartarus languisheth,
Nor do Hell's waters roll their wonted sulph'rous waves,
Nor doth Hell's furnace raise its lambent tongues of flame,
Nor doth Hell's wailing cry, dismally echoing,
Break the tranquility of their sad prison house
Who, in their respite time, revel exultingly.

IX

And we, with holy joy, keep vigil all that night;
And all the livelong night we lift our hands to God,
And pray, and vow, and weep, and watch the whole night through,
And at Thine Altar, Lord, we break the Bread of Life.
Behold a goodly sight,—a hundred flames of gold
Drawn up by pliant cords unto the vaulted roof,
Which, fed by luscious oil, through clearest crystal, beam
Like God's own firmament upon a summer's night,—
When, at some clear still time the twin Triones blink,
And, where his chariot drives the yoke of Lucifer,
The very Heavens glow, all strewn with starry sheen,
And shine and scintillate in mellow purple light.
O comely Victim which, when falls the evening dew,
To Thee most gracious God Thy grateful people give!
O Light than which no grace more precious God bestows!
O very glorious Light, which lighteneth all the rest!
Light of mine eyes art Thou, Light of mine intellect,

O holy, healing, piercing, penetrating Light!
Receive this flaming torch which I, Thy servant, humbly tend,
O Lord omnipotent, Through Thine anointed Son,
In Whom—Man's Chief—to men Thy glory stands reveal'd,
Who, from Thy Father's Heart breatheth the Paraclete,
Through Whom splendour, honour, laud, wisdom, excellence,
Goodness, and tender love make Thy great rule endure
In Threefold Majesty, whilst endless ages run.

ON GOING TO REST

I

Come Thou Most High Creator,
Whose Face no eyes have gazed on,
Come Christ Word of the Father,
Come gentle kindly Spirit.
O God of God begotten,
O God from both proceeding,
O Trinity stupendous,
One Light, one Life, one Power.

II

'Tis past the day's stern travailing,
The hour of rest returneth,
And sleep once more alluring,
Sings softly to the weary,
Whilst hearts storm-tossed and throbbing,
By care's sharp arrows smitten,
Drink deep from pale Night's chalice
The nectar of oblivion.
Its lethal force caressing
Now creeps o'er all the senses,
Nor suffereth pain's sick anguish
To rack their weary acheing.
This law by God's commandment
To man's frail form was given,

That sleep's soft healing pleasure
Might temper toil and weakness.

III

But whilst kind Rest embracing
Steals thus o'er all the body,
Bedewing with her kisses
Dull eyelids ripe for slumber,
The soul set free—unshackled,
Flies swiftly through the heavens,
Sees shapes and forms and phantoms,
And hidden things in visions.
Her origin is heaven,
E'en Œthra's purest glory.
Set free from earthly trammels,
She knows nor rest nor slumber,
But fashions many fantasies,
In form and figure varied,
By means of which to conjure
A semblance of thin action,
And calls up countless phantasms,
To flee from them in terror.
Anon God's splendour guides her,
Of things which will be, teaching,
More often lying spectres,
Of things which are not, preaching,
Deceive with black evasion,
Make sick with shrieking horror.
For some lead lives so blameless,
Their steps are scarce found tripping,
On such God's clear light shineth,
Revealing hidden mysteries;

And some have stained their being,
Polluted with sin's habit;
Such souls see signs portentous—
Are made the sport of panic.

IV

All this our Patriarch teacheth,
Laid low in noisome prison,
Interpreting their fantasies
For either courtly eunuch—
One is restored to favour
And holds the royal wine-cup,
Whilst on a cross the other
Gives meat to famished vultures—
Forewarning Pharoe's bounty,
Confused with fevered dreaming,
So store up corn in plenty,
To save the land from famine.
Anon made prince and leader,
He'll rule o'er Egypt's borders,
And share the royal sceptre,
And dwell in lordly mansions.

V

O secrets deep, tremendous,
Unutterable, holy,
Which to His chosen comrades
The Christ in dreams revealeth.
Evangelist most trusty,
Who on thy Master's bosom
Didst rest thy virgin temples,
Beyond earth's cloud-girt halo,

Thy keen eyes now see clearly
Things which before were hidden :—
The Lamb Himself empurpled
With price of man's redemption,
Who only can lay open
The book which tells what will be ;
Whose arm of mighty puissance,
A two-edged sword makes threatening—
Keen symbol of His judgment,
The first and second reckoning,
For He alone is arbiter
Of body and of spirit,
And yet a mild avenger,
Most sweet and just and gentle,
Who sends to endless exile
But few of the unholy.
To Him the Eternal Father,
A glorious name hath given,
A name at which all creatures bow,
In earth, or hell, or Heaven.
" Thy throne, O God, endureth,
For ever and for ever,
Unending Thy Dominion."
Thus spake the world's Creator.
Behold the valiant champion,
Who in His death throes conquer'd,
Who crushed the infernal dragon,
And from his gory talons,
'Neath fell Charybdis' whirlpool,
Redeemed a noble trophy,
Whilst to Hell's lowest chasm,
He speeds his vanquish'd footsteps.
With such-like dreams and dreaming

John, hero, soothed his bosom,
And wandered in the Spirit,
E'en to the seventh Heaven.

VI

For us whom frequent lapses,
And love of vice inherent,
Do mar and taint and tarnish,
Such dreams are all too holy.
Enough if tranquil slumber
Refresh our worn-out bodies.
Enough if no fell vampire
Outspread his chilling pinions.

VII

O child of God, remember
The font's baptismal washing,
The white robe which He gave thee,
The dew of thine anointing.
And when kind sleep invites thee,
Ere seeking her embraces,
First sign thy breast and forehead
With Christ's redemptive symbol.
All evil flies before it,
Naught can withstand its power,
Signed with that sign, the spirit
Rests unmoved, tranquil, holy.

VIII

Avaunt, avaunt, vain omens,
Foul ghosts of prowling passions,
Avaunt thou vile enchantress,

And cease thine incantations.
O tortuous wily serpent,
Who by thy curs'd meand'ring,
And flexuous frauds and fantasies,
Dost ulcerate calm reason.
Begone, for Christ is with us.
E'en Christ is here,—swift, vanish.
His sign right well thou knowest,
The sign which damns thy legions.

IX

Now, for a little season,
Kind Sleep shall rain soft kisses,
And fold thee in her bosom,
And lull thee with embraces;
But even mid thy dreaming
Christ's memory shall not perish,
His love thy heart shall cherish,
E'en though Night's cup be lethal.

A SONG FOR THOSE WHO FAST

I

WORD of the Father, Light of Bethlem, Nazarene,
Thou whom a maiden bore in holy purity,
Great Christ be with us in our chaste frugality,
O King serene look down on us with Thy kind eyes,
And make our fasting glad, a willing sacrifice.

II

Than this great myst'ry there is naught, forsooth, more pure,
It expiates the inmost malice of the heart,
By it the warring flesh is curbed, and tamed, and stilled,
Lest luxury should find a home for wantonness,
Should cloud and dim the vision of a strangled soul.

By it both pomp and greed are brought beneath the yoke,
And shameful sloth, the pampered child of dreams and wine,
And sordid joys, and jests unseemly and profane;
And all the varying plagues of languid sentiment
Subdued, make known the sovereign sway of abstinence.

For if to things of sense man freely gives the rein,
If fast and discipline the will do not restrain,
It often happens that the love of noble hearts :—
That flickering flame of charity, pressed down by earth,
Burns low; that drowsiness creeps o'er the sluggish soul.

Then let all fleshly whims be duly kept in check,
And let chaste prudence sit enthroned within thy breast,
E'en so, the mind with keener sight shall rise to Heaven,
The soul with swifter flight shall lift herself to God,—
More fitly hold sweet converse with the Lord of all.

III

By these and such like means that aged man of God,
The arid desert's guest, Elijah, grew in grace,
Removed and far away from noise and strife and din,
He dwelt alone with holy Silence for his bride;
And thus he shunned, they say, a multitude of sin.

But soon there came a chariot drawn by fiery steeds,
Which mounting upwards, like swift flames in winter time,
E'en bore him straight to heaven, lest earth should breathe on him
The fell contagion of her dross; disturb a soul
Whom prayer, and alms, and abstinence had rendered pure.

IV

Though Moses was God's friend and trusty messenger,
He ne'er could gaze upon the sevenfold heaven's Chief
Until the sun had steered his course amid the stars,—
Had risen and had sunk to rest full forty times,
And all that while had seen him lacking meat and drink.

And to him, praying, tears alone were nourishment.
For keeping watch each night, he lay upon the ground,
And kissed the dust which he had watered with his grief,
Until he heard the Voice of God addressing him,
And feared a glistering Light, too pure for man to see.

V

And no less mighty in this glorious art was John,
Who went before the Son of the Eternal God,
To shape o'er hill and vale a highway for His Feet,
To make the crooked paths for Him a smooth, straight road,
To root the thistles out and cast away the stones.

For well the Seer knew that God was drawing nigh,
That Christ's dear Countenance was soon to shine on man.
And so he filled the vales, and made the mountains low,
Lest Truth, descending to this earth, should there naught find
Save some rough stony by-way choked with weeds and stones.

Unwonted was the manner of his birth. A late
Unlooked-for child was he, who came when ev'ry hope
Of bearing seed had long since fled his parents' breasts,
Nor did his mother bring him forth until he'd preached
Our Queen's maternity, and that her Child was God.

And when he grew a man, he to the desert land,
Where no tree tends in summer time its grateful shade,
Nor flower thrusts its fragrant head above the sand,
Withdrew his youth, and clothed himself in skins of beasts,
Lest city-life should stain his virgin innocence.

And there with holy Abstinence he tamed his flesh,
Denied himself all meat and drink till eventide,
Till sable night had cast her shadow o'er the plain,
And then he only took a little nourishment—
A scanty meal of locusts and wild honeycombs.

He of the new Salvation was the first to speak,
For in the sacred stream that waters Chanaan
He washed away the black disgrace of inborn sin,
And when he thus his penitents had purified,
God's spirit filled their hearts with rays of heavenly light.

Then, as a vein of purest gold by fire refined
Doth glow and glister in its new-born loveliness,
Or as the fairest light of silv'ry metal cleans'd
Doth shine and scintillate, so shone those new-born souls
Whom he had cleansed from sin in Jordan's healing flood.

VI

I'll hymn thee now the glory of an old-world fast,
As Holy Writ in faithful words doth hand it down.
I'll tell thee how God's Mercy saved a death-doomed town,
How Prayer and holy Abstinence reversed its lot,
And brought to very naught the consequence of sin.

For there was once a race puffed up by wealth and might,
And through their land a canker ran of luxury;
For ev'ry soul at Nineveh was steeped in self,
And hate, and greed, and cruel lust there ruled supreme;
And, then, as often happens, Faith withdrew her light,
And Hope and Love fled too, and men forgot to pray.

At length their cup of wickedness was very full,
And God's Kind Heart was grieved at sight of so much ill,
And with a flaming sword He armed His Righteous Might,
For sin must be aveng'd, and deeds of wrong set right—
And yet He stayed His Hand in pity at their plight—

Withheld the threatened blow, and, for a little while,
Unexecuted let His uttered sentence stand,
E'en until they had had some time for penitence,
Lest, now, at last, perchance, they'd show a will to mend
Their evil ways, and break the bonds of luxury.

And so the gentle Judge raised up a messenger,
And bid him go and warn them of their pending doom.
But Jonah was a stern, proud man, and knowing well
That God would rather bless than blame, e'en save than strike,
In shame rebelled, and fled until he reached the coast;

And finding there a mighty ship for Tharsus bound,
Embarked therein, and stealthily put out to sea.
But soon a storm arose which threatened instant death:
The mariners cast lots the cause thereof to tell,
And on the prophet's head the fatal number fell.

Of all that crew, but one alone was doomed to die,
The man whose guilt the shaken urn had testified,
Him, then, they headlong threw into the raging tide.
So calmed the sea. But in His pity, God prepared
A fish, whose huge jaws closed o'er Jonah's struggling form,

Whose greedy throat gulped down his breathless, trembling flesh.
But wond'rous to relate the prophet did not die,
For gliding down the centre of the monster's tongue,
He spurned the fruitless grinding of his bloodless teeth,
Reached whole the cavern which the mighty flanks enclosed.

And there for three long days and nights he stayed,
And all that while, half stifled by the noisome heat,
Half mad with sickening fear, he blindly groped his way
Along the windings of that gruesome living maze,
And sought in vain some outlet from such misery,

Till, on the third night, with a straining, deep-drawn sob,
There where the surf is broken on the murmuring shore,
And where the glistening foam doth kiss the rocks away,
Leviathan did cast him forth, e'en living still,
And marvelling that he is still alive, once more
Can see, with tender eyes, the dawning light of day.

Then to the men of Nineveh with hastening steps
He sped, compelled thereto by God's Almighty Hand,
And sternly chid them for their deeds of infamy.
" The great Avenger's sword is hovering o'er the land,
His righteous wrath shall swiftly burn up Nineveh,
Believe my words," e'en thus he spake, and went his way

Until he reached a neighbouring mountain's rugged peak,
There, 'neath a knotted gourd, he waited for the end,
And thought to hear anon the city's startled shriek,
And smell the smoke, and see the blood-red flames dart up,
And all its halls, and homes, and squalid huts laid low,—
Wrapt in one common mass of seething misery.

But when the menaced state had learnt its pending doom,
O how they feared! All Nineveh turned out that night
Into the streets, and swarmed upon the city walls,
And groups of men with bated breath discussed the news,
And youths turned pale, and women wept, and terror reigned.

" Perchance by public fasts Christ's wrath can be appeased,"
So some one said: and no man tasted bite or sup,
And stately matrons laid aside their broidered robes
For mean attire, and letting down their flowing hair
Put dust upon their heads, instead of pearls and gold.

And men of rank girt on the clothes of common folk,
And all the vulgar throng put sackcloth on their loins,
And noble girls with hair shirts vext their tender flesh,
And hid their high-born grace with dingy mourning veils,
And school-boys left their sports, and knew not how to play.

The king tore off the brooch which clasped his robe of state,—
All sewn with emeralds, and seed pearls white as milk,
And to the squalid earth its purple lustre fell.
And then he plucked the royal crown from off his brow,
And sprinkled fœtid dust upon his perfumed hair.

And no man thought to eat, and no man thought to drink,
Though choicest viands lay upon his well-spread board
And even new-born children cried in vain for milk,
And made their little pillows wet with scalding tears,
For chilling fear had frozen every mother's breast.

And herdsmen from the country side, egged on by fear,
Penned up in fold and stall the cattle and the sheep,
Lest they should range abroad and crop the dewy grass,
Or slake their burning thirst in some cool murmuring stream,
So break the Fast. And thus they wailed in empty stalls,
And one great cry of agony went up to Heav'n.

Jehovah heard it, and His short-lived anger fled,
And lovingly He changed the sin'ster oracle,
For if the sinner pleads, God easily forbears;
The debtor's cry for grace His mercy swiftly hears,
And when His children weep, He wipes away their tears.

VII

But why example seek from times long past away,
When Jesus, Whom the Prophet called Emmanuel,—
God with us, that is, living still,—but yesterday,
Though weighed down by the weakness of man's sorry flesh,
With gladsome heart for man's dear sake did penitence.

Man's fragile form, by nature weak, soft delicate,
So prone to bend the knee 'neath sin's caressing yoke,
The Christ by stern endurance freed and fortified,
Smote from the yielding neck the bonds of luxury,
And bound in fetters, lust, who tyrannised before.

For in the lonely desert-land He lay concealed,
And fasted there for forty days and forty nights,
'Twas thus the God-Man comforted, heal'd, cheer'd, made glad,
Poor Adam's fallen flesh, erst frail, and sick, and sad,
Through vainly seeking peace in self and soft delights.

But Satan, when he saw a thing built up of clay
So long enduring such great toil was sore amazed,
And sought with cunning wiles to solve the mystery,
" Perchance," said he, " 'tis God arrayed in human flesh,"
And, when he knew the truth, he turned his back and fled.

VIII

Then let us follow, each one of us, as each one can,
The holy rule which Christ's example sanctified ;—
Which He—Our Lord and Chief—to His disciples gave.
So, like a queen who bendeth all things to her will,
The spirit triumphing, shall rule the feeble flesh.

Behold a sword which filleth Satan's soul with gall ;—
A weapon which the Lord of heaven and earth approves,
Which fits the heart to welcome Sacrificial Grace,
Which wakes the sluggish will to acts of Faith and Love,
Which purgeth from the breast the impure slough of sin.

The tiny spark, which some stray blast hath cast into
A mighty river's flood, is not more swiftly quenched,
Nor doth the snow more swiftly melt beneath the sun,
Than flees the scurvy crew of unclean wickedness,
When Mother Abstinence and Charity draw nigh.

To clothe the naked, and to give the hungry meat,
To proffer kindly aid to all men in distress,
To hold in like esteem the mighty and the meek,
Regarding neither wealth, nor birth, nor lofty state.
These are thine attributes, O comely Charity !
O Charity, how God-like is thy wide embrace !

How blest the man who taketh thee for his fair bride,
Who, for thy love, doth lavish on thee all his hoard,
And keep close secret where he hides his treasured gold !
Eternal wealth shall be the lot of such an one,
For fruit an hundred fold doth bless God's usurers.

AFTER FASTING

Christ, of thy servants' lives the rule and pattern,
Thou who with gentle reins dost lead and guide us,
Sweetly restraining, and with light hand curbing
    Them that obey thee.

Thou, who whilst weighed down by man's fragile body
Didst lend Thy back to bear a mighty burthen,
And for his neck didst weave a yoke of roses,
    So to entice him.

Sun's rays are lowered mid the azure heaven,
Of his swift course, he now hath run three stages,
To us one fourth part of his light remaineth,
    'Tis the ninth hour.

We, of our brief vow, now have paid the off'ring,
And, of Christ's goodness, meat is set before us,
And we partake with glad hearts of His bounty,
    Duly rejoicing.

For this the Master is so sweet and gracious,
For this the teacher with soft words doth feed us,
That His light yoke should soothe our weary shoulders,
    Sore with sin's burthen.

But, lest with downcast looks and tearful eyelids,
Some should thus think to make themselves look mournful,
That all the world may know that they are fasting,
  Jesus forewarns us.

" When ye do penance, tend," he saith, " the body,
" So shall the life blood tinge thy ruddy visage,
" And deathly pallor shall not mar its beauty,
  " Telling thy secret."

Then, with glad blushes, hide the deadly conflict,
When self, for Christ's sake, thou dost tame and conquer,
God saw thee fighting, though from man 'twas hidden,
  And will reward thee.

He is the shepherd, vigilant and trusty,
Who sought the sick lamb, weary, tattered, footsore,
When it was straying in death's gloomy forest,
  Shut out from Eden.

Who, when He found it, laid it on His shoulders—
Hell's cruel sleuth-hounds crouching low before Him—
And healed, and healthful, to the sunny sheepfold
  Safely restored it.

To that green field where grows the tend'rest herbage,
Where no rude bramble waves its thorny branches,
Where no rough thistle arms its seed with spear-heads,
  Needle-like piercing.

Where 'neath cool palm groves grass is flecked with lilies,
And where the laurel bends its glossy foliage
O'er gurgling fountains, gushing forth pure water,
  Clearer than crystal.

O gentle Shepherd, tender, kind, and faithful,
No thanks can measure Thy deep heart's vast pity,
And the great price of Adam's re-instation,
    None can repay Thee.

E'en though we chasten by stern fast and vigil
This frame of weakness, of free choice contemning
All that doth cherish, recreate, and comfort
    Man's fallen body.

Our puny penance, though it be untiring,
Can never equal Christ's stupendous labour,
And when the earthen vase is used too hardly,
    At length, it breaketh.

Lest, then, the blood should turn to wat'ry pallor,
And all their strength should quit these fragile ashes,
Whose frail embrace could, thus, scarce hold the spirit
    Struggling for freedom.

Broad is the maxim, and most light and easy,
Which Mother Church proposes to her children,
So that each one may pay the debt of fasting
    As he is able.

This doth suffice—if thou 'fore every action
Do first invoke the will of God Almighty,
Thus shalt thou eat, and thus refrain from eating,
    All for His glory.

So shalt thou lift thy heart from earth to heaven,
So shall Christ bless the good gifts He bestoweth,
So shall they be for thee a source of blessing
    Freely awarded.

O may the food which Thy kind hand hath given
For the refreshment of this fragile body,
Nourish alike the heart, and feed the spirit,
    Gracious provider.

AT THE BURIAL OF THE DEAD

I

O GOD, fiery Fountain of Spirits,
Great Father whence floweth all being,
Who, taking quick life and dead matter,
Didst build up a Man to Thy liking.

Of each part, Lord, Thou art the Ruler,
Thou, Lord, art the Leash of their joining,
For Thee, whilst they cling to each other,
Both Body and Spirit are living.

But, when Thy Hand rends them asunder,
The creature Man falleth to nothing,
The dry earth drinks in his dead body,
The heavens absorb his soul's being.

Be the woof woven never so stoutly,
Time's fingers unravel its threadings.
Be fetters forged never so firmly,
Time solveth, at length, their cohering.

'Tis the stern lot of all things created
To fail and to fade and to perish,
But Christ's Love slays Death for His children,
And gives Him a new child to cherish,

And shows them how Man's royal spirit,
Which came forth directly from Heaven,
Though bound in the chains of Earth's bondage,
Can still sway the sceptre and govern.

II

If, haply, an earthly will relish
The things of this earth and earth's squalour,
O'erwhelmed by the weight of its grossness
The soul shall sink down with the body.

But if, mindful of her high lineage,
She shunneth all sinful contagion,
The bride shall give wings to the bridegroom
And fly with him even to Heaven.

For the form which lies lifeless before us
Shall one day awake from its slumber,
The soul shall come back at God's bidding
To dwell with her lost love for ever.

Yet a little while and life's quick fire
Shall make these cold embers all glowing,
Yet a little while, and the red blood
Shall give them new grace in its flowing.

This lead corse which lies stiff, and rigid,
And rotting within its dark prison,
Shall soon take to itself wings of silver
And soar like a fair dove to Heaven.

III

'Tis for this that the graves of our comrades
Are so carefully watched o'er and tended,
'Tis for this, that to dry husks and ashes
Such homage and honour are render'd.

'Tis for this that we meetly array them
In linen the finest and fairest,
Embalm them with myrrh and sweet incense,
And perfumes the choicest and rarest.

And what is the tale which they tell us,
These monuments, graved in white marble?
"We cherish," they whisper, "a something
Not dead, but wrapt in sweet slumber."

"Our stones, deftly hewn out and chiselled,
Betoken the faith of Christ's giving,
This numbed seed, which winter hath shrivelled,
Shall burst in the Spring to new living."

Whosoe'er then in love and in pity
Shall do this last act for a brother
Doth show himself kind, in the first place,
To Jesus his Lord and Creator.

And next on himself hath he pity,
For all men are one in this sorrow.
King Death, who to-day greets thy comrade,
Will welcome thee surely to-morrow.

IV

Tobias was seated at table,
His servants were waiting to serve him,
When somebody whispered "a dead man
Lies without in the highway unburied."

Then, straightway he went forth to seek him
And carried him home to his chamber,
And laid him at night in earth's bosom,
And wept for him as for a brother.

And God for the old man's great pity,
Had pity on him in his sadness,
And touching with gall his dim eyeballs,
He turned all his grief into gladness.

V

In this story the world's Father shows us
How bitter and sharp is the healing
Which sheddeth o'er dark souls new daylight,
Which giveth to blind hearts new seeing.

We learn too, that there's no road to Heaven
But that which all rugged and thorny
Leads at last through the pathway of darkness,
Through the chill shade of Night's mist-clad valley.

But, take heart, Christian soul, and be joyful,
Bethink thee the end of thy journey,
That after the tempest comes sunshine,
That Death is the gateway of Heaven,

That the frame that was racked with pain's sickness,
In the life after death, feels no sorrow,
Knows not what it is to be weary,
Rejoiceth for ever and ever.

That the cheek that was careworn and hollow,
Where suff'ring had set his grey pallor,
Is more fair now than lilies in springtime,
More radiant, than roses in summer.

Old age cannot wither its beauty,
Nor furrow the peace of that calm brow,
Nor lessen, nor weigh down, nor shatter,
Nor shrivel with time's wasting fever.

For sickness, and death, and disorder,
O'erwhelmed by the weight of Christ's mercy,
In like kind with the coin which we paid them,
Pay the debt of their own expiation.

Whilst the flesh, now made whole and immortal,
Enthroned in the grace of God's glory,
Beholds them afar off bewailing
The woes which were once its companions.

VI

Why mourn for the dead then so sadly?
Why rend thy poor heart-strings with crying?
Why combat the will of thy Father?
Why question his merciful ruling?

Now hushed be all mournful complaining,
Let tears dry on the cheek of the mother,
Let no man bewail love's lost pledges,
This Death is Life's grand reparation.

For the dry seed to earth's care entrusted,
Shall at length burst the bars of its prison,
And shoot out again from the green sward
A stem, and a leaf, and a blossom.

VII

O Mother Earth cherish and tend it,
Embrace it in thy gentle bosom,
'Tis the form of a man that I give thee,
An ark of gold, battered and broken,

Which once was the home of a spirit,
By the word of God formed and created.
Within the courts of this temple
The Christ's Holy Wisdom once rested.

Then shelter the body I bring thee,
For God is the Lord of its being,
'Tis His creature, made to His image,
And one day at thy hand He will seek it.

Glad times of refreshment are coming
When God shall merge hope in fruition;
Then, then, shalt thou open thy bosom
And give Him the man I now give thee.

For even though Time's patient fingers
Should crumble these dry bones to powder,
So that but the scant mede of a handful
Could compass the bulk of their ashes.

If the winds and the waters embrace them
And scatter them hither and thither,
Be it so, this frail form shall not perish,
God knoweth the home of its essence.

VIII

But until, O my God, Thou dost call back,
And re-form the clay of this body,
To what land wilt Thou send the lone spirit,
Bereft of her friend and companion?

Shall she lie on the bosom of Abram
Like the soul of the beggar, whom Dives,
Afar off, saw hemmed in with flowers,
Until the glad day of refreshment?

We trust to Thy word, O Redeemer,
Who when with pale Death Thou wast wrestling,
Didst cry out to the thief, 'mid the combat,
To follow Thee where Thou shouldst lead him.

Behold now the highway lies open
Which leads to the broad plains of Eden,
And Man may again hold the garden
Of which Satan's spite had despoiled him.

L—2

Then bid that this soul be made holy,
Great Chief, in the land of her forming,
In the place where she first was created,
In the home which she left for earth's wandering.

And the buried shrine we will cherish,
And strew violets o'er it, and roses,
And with the sweet scent of their fragrance
Our prayers too shall mount up to Heaven.

A CHRISTMAS CAROL

I

Why doth the sun his straitened path
Now hastening towards us thus desert?
Hath Christ come down to dwell on earth
And make the way of light more large?

How swiftly hath the shrunken day
Rolled by of late her fleeting grace,—
Pale flickering torch, almost extinct,
So wanly burnt its feeble flame.

Now shall the sky wax roseate,
And Mother Earth exultant shout,
Aurora mounteth, step by step,
The orbit of her pristine course.

II

Arise, arise, sweet Lucifer,
Thou Advocate of twofold race,
Whom Holy Chastity herself,
Brings forth in all her virgin grace.

God is Thy puissant origin,
His lips the Source whence Thou dost flow,
And yet from all eternity,
O Wisdom, in His Heart wast Thou.

God's Wisdom uttered, reared the sky,
The earth and every other thing,
All by His Word's great might was made,
Because His Word was very God.

III

But when from forth chaotic Night,
He'd called the germs and seeds of things—
He, their great Lord and Architect—
And set each creature in its place,

Back to His Father's breast He sped,
And rested in His heart, until
Ten thousand times a thousand years,
Had rolled the circuit of its course—

Till He, God's Holy One, was grieved,
At sight of such long wickedness,
For Satan by his cunning wiles,
Had harnessed Adam to his yoke—

Was driving him at headlong speed,
To his dread home in Tartarus,
And, jeeringly, had made him think,
That fetiches could set him free—

That gods of wood, and brass, and stone,
Could soothe and 'suage and sympathize.
And sin had tainted everything,
And all God's earth was sick to death.

And Jesu's kind heart could not bear
To see His noble handiwork
Which He Himself had made so fair,
A blighted, broken, shattered wreck.

And so He girt on Adam's garb,
That He might raise him from the tomb,
And break death's yoke from off his neck,
And bring him back again to God.

IV

This is the festal day, on which
Thy Father breathed in Thee a soul,
And put on Thee a robe of flesh,
And linked together God and man.

V

Didst recognize, O noble maid,
All through the weary waiting time,
That Motherhood increased in thee
The glory of thy virgin pride?

O how great treasure rich and rare
In that sealed casket lieth hid!
God's token of a golden age,
And new-born joy for all mankind.

VI

At length the longed-for hour has come,
Hark to the musick of those tears!
The Sun of Righteousness bursts forth,
Foul winter changes into spring.

Methinks that day glad Mother Earth,
Flecked all her fields with fairest flowers,
That e'en the desert's breath grew sweet
With roses and with violets.

That every dour and barren thing—
Dry parched-up rock, and thirsty stone,
Then changed the nature of its heart,
Paid passing homage to the Child,—

Brought forth mid beds of velvet moss,
In opening leaves and unfurled fronds,
A wealth of loveliness untold.
That honey flowed from every crag,

And spikenard from the tamarisk,
And balsam from the seer gnarled oak,
And all the land breathed blessedness.
How holy is Thy manger bed,

Eternal King of Israel!
All nations shall throughout all time
Adore the stall where Thou didst sleep,
Where low in adoration knelt

Before Thee, ox, and ass, and sheep.
Lo, hastening with eager steps
The strangest throng that ere was seen,
A crowd of simple shepherd folk,

Followed by all their bleating flock,
And Pagan chiefs from far off lands
With all their savage retinue—
Huge untamed soulless animals,

Of mighty mien, and grand physique;
And when they saw the sleeping child,
They all fell down and worshipped Him.
Then what was foolish was made wise,

And what was squalid, purified,
And what was bestial, humanized,
And what was soulless, sanctified;
They knelt down brutes, and rose up men.

VII

The dumb ox knows his owner's crib,
The patient ass her Master's stall,
But Israel doth not perceive,
My people will not understand.

A little town, a lowly inn,
A stable, and a manger bed,
A Virgin, and a feeble Child,
These are the signs which show thy King.

Dost recognise them Israel?
Then see Him flashing through the sky,
All aurioled in rainbow light,
A million myriads round about

Waiting to do His least behest.
Behold His lightning scintillate
The awful lightning of the Cross,
And hear His thousand thunders roar

Their roll-call to the judgment seat,
With tears thou'lt recognise Him then,
Too late, too late, O Israel !
Too late to claim a Father's love,

To lay thy head upon His breast,
To ever see His gracious smile.
And this is Hell, O Israel.
Then own Him now and thou shalt see

The blessedness of His Fair Face,
And taste the sweetness of His Heart,
And weld thy will to His for Aye,
And this is Heaven, Israel.

AN EPIPHANY HYMN

I

ALL ye who seek th' anointed King,
Lift up to Heav'n your weary eyes,
See gleaming, mid its purple haze,
His token there of endless fame,
A glorious Star which pales the sun,
Outshines his beauty, shames his might,
A Herald, which proclaims to man
God's advent clothed in human flesh.
This star serves not night's sable course,
Like the pale moon, whose silver light
Doth wax and wane each month, supreme,
Day owns Him for her lord and chief.
Two sisters wend their starry way
Who never turn their eyes from earth,—
Stanch Ursa, faithful Ursula,—
But often storm clouds dim their light.
One Star alone remaineth fix'd,
One heav'nly candle burns for aye,
Nor storm, nor mist, nor night nor day
Can hide the beauty of His smile,
Can dim the lustre of one ray
Which beams from His fair face.
And those sad stars which presage death

And war, and want, and pestilence,
Now shrunk and shrivel'd melt away,
Like evil dreams at dawn of day,
Slain by his healing radiance.

II

And lo from Persia's very heart,
Whence the great sun star issueth,
Three wise men skilled in heav'nly lore
Descry Christ's banner all unfurled,
Behold before its shim'ring light
The other stars grown pale as death,
See Venus hide her loveliness,
And veil the beauty of her brow.
"Who is this mighty Chief," they say,
'Fore Whom the heavens tremble so,
Whom light and ether humbly serve,
Whom all the other stars obey?
A something brilliant we behold
Which knows no end, which cannot cease,
Interminable, grand, sublime,
Older than Heaven, or than Chaos."
" This star must be the gentile's King,
The Glory of the Jewish race,
The Prince foretold to Abraham,
And to his seed for evermore."
" For that first sower, staunch and true,
Who gave to God his one lov'd boy,
Beheld far off, with Faith's keen sight,
His seed surpassing all the stars,
And all the golden grains of sand
Which lie along earth's storm-swept shore."

"A Stem hath burst from Jesse's root,
A Bud from David's royal stock,
A Blossom very fair to see,
Which ruleth Heav'n and earth, and hell,"
Then where the star had ploughed its course,
And left athwart the azure sky
A little streak of quivering flame,
Thither they lead their eager steps.
Till Christ's great ensign rests at length
Above an Infant's lowly bed,
And bending, sheds with humbled rays,
A golden aureole round its head.
And when the Magi saw that thing,
They brought forth all their eastern gifts;
Incense, and myrrh, and shining gold,
With which the crowns of kings are made,
And falling down adored the Child.

III

O Child to whom Thy Father gave
A threefold, inborn, excellence,
Now recognise these mystic signs
Of majesty and puissant might.
The gold and Saban frankincense
Make known Thy Kingship, own Thee God,
The myrrh proclaims Thee very Man,
Foreshadowing Thy sepulchre.
That sepulchre where Thou, O God,
By laying down Thy human life
And taking up that life again
Didst burst through death's dark prison house.

IV

Of all great cities, thou alone,
Art greatest, lowly Bethlehem,
Who didst bring forth Salvation's Chief,
By heav'nly means incorporate.
O little town, thou wast the nurse,
Which nurtured God the Father's Son
His heir, true God of very God,
Made flesh by God the Paraclete.
And He Who wrote the Testament,
That Testament which Prophets signed—
His Father—gave to Him a realm,
And bade Him hold imperial sway,
A kingdom, which embraces earth,
And sea and sky—all things therein—
Which stretches out from east to west,
Ascends to Heav'n,—goes down to Hell.

V

But Herod's soul was sick with grief;
The advent of a King of Kings
To rule o'er Israel's race, and hold
King David's sceptre vexed him sore.
Till so beside himself he grew,
With gnawing fear, that summoning
His satellites, he bid them bathe
Their swords in infants' virgin blood.
"Let every male child fall," said he,
"Which hangs upon its mother's breast.
Search well their bosoms, lest perchance
Some lying jade should cheat my right—

I have no faith in Bethlehem—
And bear away her puny boy.
This King of kings, forsooth, shall die."
And so the wild fierce soldiery,
Rushed out to seek the Royal Babe,
Sheath'd deep their swords in newborn flesh,
And raging, ripp'd up children's lives.
Scarce did their little limbs afford
E'en space on which to shower blows,
Their tiny throats were narrower
Than the sharp dagger's slender girth,
So young were they, and weak, and small.
O very barbarous spectacle !
They dashed their heads on jagged stones,
And beat them till their eyes start out,
Till all their milky brains gush forth.
Or, in a dark deep pool, they throw—
All heedless of his mother's tears—
Some trembling boy, whose very sobs
Are stifled by the gurgling flow.

VI

All hail ye flowers of martyrdom,
Whom at the very dawn of light,
Christ's persecutor swept away,
Like a whirlwind rending rosebuds.
O first fruits of the battlefield !
O little soldiers slain for Christ,
O tender flock of innocents,
Play on beneath His altar throne
With martyrs' palms, and golden crowns!

VII

But all that blood was vainly shed,
And brought no peace to Herod's soul,
For 'mid the slaughter, one child lived,
Escap'd the sword which cut off hope
From ev'ry mother's heart, save one,
Throughout the land of Bethlehem.
That child was Christ, the virgin-born,
The Child whom Herod wished to slay.

VIII

So Moses, too, in days of yore,
Great saviour of his nation's life,—
Christ's office thus prefiguring—
Had foiled another tyrant's law,
An edict born of jealous fear,
Which nulled the Hebrew woman's right
To rear the token of her love,
Who travailing, should bear a son.
But spurning Pharao's tyranny,
A mother went and hid her child,
She saved his life for deeds of fame
That one day men might bless his name.
For when the child had fully grown
Jehovah took him for His priest
And gave to him all graved in stone
The written tables of the Law—
Dost thou not recognise the Christ
In that great hero typified,
Who slew the flower of Egypt's flock
And loosed the yoke from Israel?

For we, too, groaned beneath the yoke,
Pressed down by error's cruel sway,
Until our Chief crushed Satan's head,
And took death's bitter sting away.
Them, whom the Red Sea's waves had washed,
This Moses, with sweet water laved,
He pointed out the cloud of gold
Which led the way to Chanaan.
And when the battle raged below,
Uplifting both his hands to God,
Like Christ upon the blood-stained cross,
He quell'd the strength of Amalech:

IX

Behold a type more perfect still—
The conqueror whose faithful hand,
Carved out and shared the promised land,
To all the sons of Israel
When their long journeying was o'er.
Who drew from out of Jordan's bed—
That stream which 'fore God's ark had fled—
Twelve emblems apostolical,
E'en thrice four stones of solid rock.
Then rightly do the Magi own,
That they have seen the Jewish King,
The mighty deeds of those old chiefs,
So clearly Jesus typify.

X

He ord'reth all things new and old,
He is the King of all the Kings,

Which ruled o'er Israel's family.
He is the Lord of Mother Church,
Whom ev'ry race and land obey.
The sons of Effrem call him God,
With them Manassa's holy house,
And ev'ry stock whose root doth own,
The twelvefold seed by Jacob sown.
And Agar's once degenerate race,
Which followed rites unorthodox,
And whatsoever tribe had shaped
Dire Baal from the smelting pot,
Give up their fathers' smoky gods,
Of wood, and bronze, and clay, and stone,
The work of file, or knife, or saw,
To worship Jesus Christ alone.

XI

O all ye nations of the earth,
Judea, Greece, and Scythia,
Thrace, Egypt, Persia mighty Rome,
Be very glad and shout for mirth,
One King reigns o'er the universe.
Then praise the Lord ye blessed souls,
And praise Him, ye most miserable,
Let every creature which hath breath,
Proclaim and bless His Holiness,
And let the weakly ones be glad,
And e'en the dead no longer sad,
For henceforth no man tasteth death.

www.ingramcontent.com/pod-product-compliance
Lightning Source LLC
Chambersburg PA
CBHW020300090426
42735CB00009B/1165